THE
FACTS ISCARD
ABOUT

DRINKING &
DRIVING

BY
Andy Hjelmeland

EDITED BY
Laurie Beckelman

CONSULTANT
Elaine Wynne, M.A., Licensed Psychologist

CRESTWOOD HOUSE
New York

LIBRARY OF CONGRESS CATALOGING IN PUBLICATION DATA

Hjelmeland, Andy.
  Drinking and driving

  p.   cm. — (The Facts about)
  SUMMARY: Discusses the consequences of drinking and then driving, with a step-by-step
scenario of what happens to a driver who is arrested for drunk driving. Includes addresses to
write to for more information.
  1. Drinking and traffic accidents — United States — Juvenile literature. [1. Drinking and
traffic accidents.] I. Title. II. Series.
  HE5620.D7H57   1990   363.12'51—dc20   89-25406   CIP
  ISBN 0-89686-496-0   AC

PHOTO CREDITS

Cover: The Image Works: Bob Daemmrich
DRK Photo: (Don & Pat Valenti) 4; (C.C. Lockwood) 23
Photo Researchers: (Richard Hutchings) 6, 9; (Larry Mulvehill) 27; (Catherine Ursillo) 34-35;
  (Suzanne Goldstein) 41
Devaney Stock Photos: (William R. Wright) 11; 16, 42-43
AP–Wide World: 12, 29, 31
The Image Works: (Bob Daemmrich) 14, 20, 24, 30, 33, 39; (Mark Antman) 32; (Skip
  O'Rourke) 36-37

Macmillan Publishing Company
866 Third Avenue
New York, NY 10022
Collier Macmillan Canada, Inc.

CRESTWOOD HOUSE

Printed in the United States of America
First Edition
10 9 8 7 6 5 4 3 2 1

TABLE OF CONTENTS

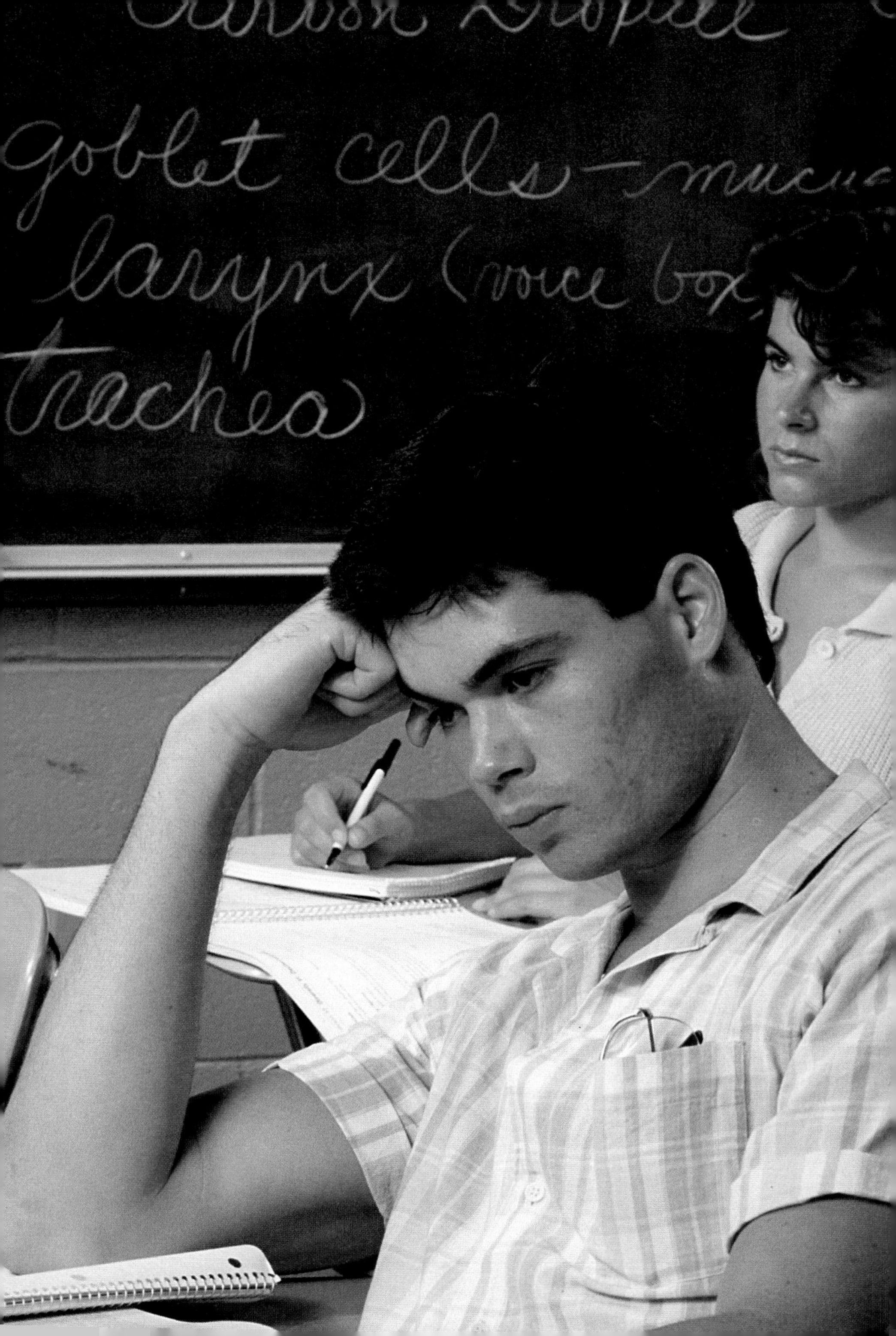
goblet cells
larynx
trachea

A NIGHT TO REMEMBER

On a cold December evening in 1988, drunk-driving victims from around the world met in St. Paul, Minnesota. They met for the International Candlelight Vigil of Remembrance and Hope. A hushed audience watched as photo after photo flashed across a large screen—infants, entire families, teens in graduation robes. All had been killed by drunk drivers. On and on, the parade of smiling, hopeful, innocent faces flickered across the screen.

Blind musicians played somber music to this endless procession of lives shortened by drunk drivers. Sight wasn't necessary in this charged atmosphere. Tears flowed as freely from the sightless as from those who could see the victims remembered at this mass memorial.

Then the living victims came to the stage.

A mother mourning the loss of her four-year-old daughter... A fourteen-year-old girl in burn bandages, survivor of a bus struck by a drunk driver. In a hoarse whisper, she read the names and ages of her 24 friends who were killed in the accident... A father whose daughter had been killed while jogging by a drunk driver... An angry woman who addressed the audience: "My mother's death was NOT an act of God. It was the act of a drunk, foolish young man."

At the end, 700 candles pierced the darkened hall, beacons of remembrance to the casualties of drunk drivers.

Each year, 24,000 people are killed in alcohol-related traffic accidents. An additional 500,000 people are burned, paralyzed, or maimed.

Smoking marijuana and snorting cocaine also impair the clear vision and quick reflexes that people need for driving.

OTHER DRUGS

Alcohol, of course, isn't the only drug that affects people's ability to drive safely. Cocaine, crack, marijuana, and other street drugs impair vision, coordination, reflexes, alertness, and judgment. So do some medicines.

6

Cough medicines, cold remedies, and sleeping pills and tablets often contain some form of amphetamine (speed). And many liquid medicines contain alcohol. That is why the warning labels often caution users not to drive motor vehicles. They also warn that the drugs may cause "drowsiness, restlessness, nervousness, sleeplessness, excitability." Driving under the influence of any drug is illegal. And dangerous.

WHY NOT DRINK AND DRIVE?

Drunk drivers kill themselves, their passengers, other motorists, and pedestrians. Each year in this country, about 24,000 people die in alcohol-related traffic accidents. That is one death every 22 minutes. Some 7,400 of those killed are innocent victims who have not been drinking. Among teenagers, traffic accidents are the leading cause of death.

Drunk drivers also maim, paralyze, burn, and scar. For every minute of every day, someone is in an alcohol-related crash. That's 525,600 people a year.

Even small amounts of alcohol affect a driver's judgment, vision, and ability to make quick, accurate decisions. In short, alcohol dulls the skills drivers need most.

In addition, the financial costs of drinking and driving are staggering. It is impossible to place a dollar amount on medical expenses, damage to property, court costs, and the time spent by police responding to and investigating alcohol-related accidents.

A drunk-driving conviction can result in a fine, jail, the loss of a driver's license, or canceled insurance. A drunken driver caught more than once or involved in an accident that causes death or serious injuries can be charged with a *felony*. A felony conviction could mean a prison sentence. Losing a job is also possible—especially if the job requires driving.

But the cost of drinking and driving is often much higher than a lost license or even time in jail. In the following story, the loss of someone special makes any other penalty unimportant.

GRADUATION NIGHT

Paul bolted upright in bed, Jenny's screams echoing in his mind. Even after two years, the nightmare was always the same. Blinding headlights, the crunch of metal...and Jenny's scream.

Until the accident, the evening had been great. Paul remembered Jenny, so beautiful in her cap and gown as she crossed the stage to receive her diploma. He was on top of the world. Graduating! Finally!

Later, there was a party, a beer, a couple of beers. He

The lives of those who survive drunk – driving accidents are never the same again – especially when their friends or families have been killed or permanently injured.

knew he had to drive but – well, a couple wouldn't hurt anything, he told himself. After all, he was 18 years old and a high school graduate. He was practically an adult. The more he drank, the less he worried about having to drive.

When he and Jenny left the party three hours later, several friends offered to drive them home. "I'm fine,"

Paul insisted. I'm not staggering or acting like a goofy drunk, he thought.

While driving, however, he realized that he wasn't sharp. When he reached an area of road construction, the flashing warning lights blurred with oncoming headlights.

"Watch out, Paul!" Jenny shouted.

Paul heard a THUNK-THUNK-THUNK as he knocked down a row of construction signs. He yanked the steering wheel hard. The car screeched across the centerline. Then came the blast of an air horn. When Paul glanced up, headlights from a truck glared through the windshield. That's when Jenny screamed.

The day after the accident, Paul woke up in the hospital. His head ached. Pains shot through his body. But he would be okay, the nurses told him. He was lucky.

And Jenny? They wouldn't say. Later in the day, his minister told him gently: Jenny had been thrown against the windshield. She had been killed instantly.

Paul recovered fully—except for the nightmares.

HOW MUCH IS TOO MUCH?

How much can someone drink and still drive safely? The answer isn't simple. It varies from person to person and for the same person at different times. The amount of

Drinking that takes place in cars – at tailgate parties before football games or while cruising – may invite trouble.

alcohol in the blood, not the number of drinks, determines if someone is drunk. Police use this *blood-alcohol level* to decide if someone is *legally drunk*.

If a police officer suspects a driver of drinking, he or she may ask the driver to perform a *field sobriety test*. This test might be walking a straight line. It might be touching the tip of the nose with the point of an index finger or counting backward from ten. These simple tests measure coordination and alertness. The police may also ask the driver to blow into the mouthpiece of a breath tester. The breath tester measures the percentage of alcohol in the blood.

Police use both these tests to decide if a driver is drunk and should be arrested. Certain medical conditions, such as diabetic reactions, show symptoms similar to drunk-

A woman demonstrates the use of a computerized breath tester, which will measure the amount of alcohol in her blood.

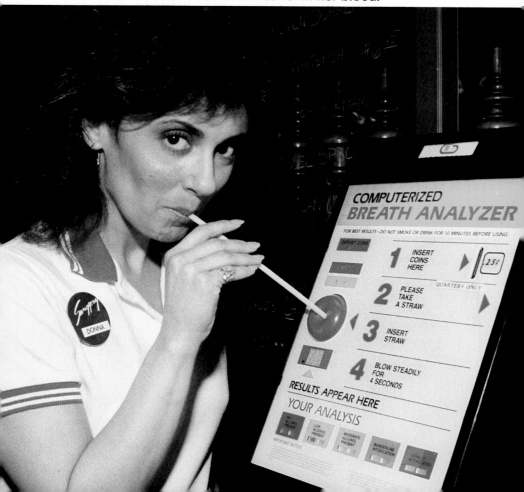

enness. Before making an arrest, police want to be sure any odd behavior is due to drinking, not illness.

A reading of .10 or higher on the breath tester means the driver is legally drunk. He or she will be arrested. A driver who refuses to take the breath test automatically loses his or her license under the *implied-consent law.* Under this law, when you receive a driver's license, you are giving your consent (even though you may not know it) to be tested at any time for blood-alcohol percentage. It is "implied."

An arrested driver may face further testing. He or she may be taken to a hospital, where trained personnel will analyze blood and urine samples. At the police station, the driver may be given another breath test, this time with a *Breathalyser.* This is a larger and more accurate machine than the *preliminary breath tester (PBT)* used earlier. Again, a reading of .10 or higher means the driver is legally *intoxicated*—drunk. In some states, a reading between .05 and .10 means the driver is legally *impaired.* Some states will arrest a driver with a lower reading under a Driving While Ability Impaired law. This is usually a less serious offense.

What does all this mean? How much can someone drink before reaching this magic number, this .10 blood-alcohol level? It depends. A large person has more body area in which to absorb the alcohol. Two people can drink the same amount, but it will affect the larger person more slowly. A full stomach also slows down alcohol's journey into the bloodstream. So does sipping a drink slowly

rather than "chugging." The faster someone drinks, the faster he or she will get drunk.

Without a breath tester, it is impossible to tell the percentage of alcohol in the blood. And even a breath test gives only the legal limit. It doesn't tell whether or not someone can drive safely. An inexperienced drinker with a .05 reading may be noticeably drunk. A heavy drinker, on the other hand, may show no outward sign of drunkenness with a .10 blood-alcohol reading.

The only safe decision is to drink no alcohol before driving. Any amount has an effect, even on the best drivers.

RUNNING THROUGH MOLASSES

Imagine the fastest human in the world running in molasses. Now take a professional race-car driver—the winner, say, of the Indianapolis 500. Get him or her drunk.

The effect would be similar. Why? Because the more someone drinks, the slower that person's reflexes become.

When someone sneaks up behind you and yells "Boo!" you immediately jump. That is a *reflex action.* It requires no thought. You simply act. That is the body's protective response to danger.

Quick reflexes are needed when driving a car. A car may stop suddenly in front of you. A small child may dash into

These college students set up an elaborate hose and funnel device for pouring beer into their mouths. The faster they drink, the faster they will get drunk.

15

the street from between two parked cars. Drivers must react immediately.

You're strolling through the park. To your right, something—you don't know what—swoops down at you from the sky. You instantly duck and cover your head. It's only an angry bird letting you know you're too close to its nest. Your *peripheral vision* picked up the nose-diving bird. Peripheral

Drinking limits a person's ability to see objects to the left and right of the body. It also slows down a driver's ability to brake and steer.

vision is the area surrounding our direct line of sight.

People lose peripheral vision when they drink. They develop *tunnel vision*. That's why a drunk staggering down the street looks like a toddler learning to walk. The person walks with head down, eyes focused only a few feet ahead, because peripheral vision is gone. Alcohol also lessens sensitivity to colors, including red. The ability to estimate speed and distance of objects is impaired, as is resistance to glare.

Now imagine putting someone who is drunk behind the wheel of 2,000 pounds of steel capable of traveling 90 or 100 miles per hour.

A BIKING TRAGEDY

When Cathy opened the door, she saw a new ten-speed bicycle standing inside the porch. A birthday card hung from the handlebars by a yellow ribbon.

"Happy 14th, Cathy!" it said. The card was signed by each member of her family. She smiled as she read her five-year-old brother's crudely printed crayon lettering, "**Happy Buyking From Billy.**"

Cathy rode her bike every day. She especially loved riding around the lake near her home. Her girlfriend Susan, also had a ten-speed, and they often rode together.

One warm June day, they met two boys on the bike trail

that circled the lake. Soon, the four of them were meeting every afternoon. Susan began teasing Cathy about one of the boys. "You like him, don't you?"

"Who?"

"Ha-ha. Like you don't know who I mean. He's practically your boyfriend."

Cathy grinned. "How about you and what's-his-name?"

They both giggled.

On the Fourth of July, they all agreed to meet at a nearby park. Cathy spent a long time in front of the mirror before leaving the house. She wanted to look nice for Jeff — her almost boyfriend.

It was a beautiful, sunny afternoon when she biked down the street toward Susan's house. Thoughts of summer filled her mind: no school for two months, sleeping late, playing softball, biking with a cute almost boyfriend.

Two blocks from Susan's house, a pickup truck suddenly raced out of an alley. It caught Cathy full force, throwing her against the curb on the opposite side of the street. Her twisted bicycle lay under the truck. A crowd quickly gathered. Sirens and flashing red lights soon followed.

Cathy's spine was permanently damaged. Unless a miracle occurred, she would never walk, ride a bike, or swim again. In fact, she wouldn't do much of anything without assistance. She would be confined to a wheelchair.

The driver of the pickup was a 22-year-old alcoholic

named Nancy. At the trial, her husband testified that she had been drinking all day.

WHEN A DRINKING DRIVER GETS CAUGHT

Jim was returning from a picnic. He'd had five, maybe six beers in four hours. But he didn't feel drunk. He'd been active – eating, swimming, and playing volleyball. Behind the wheel, he was alert and in control.

Up ahead he saw a roadblock. Several police cars were parked along the shoulder of the road. As each car stopped, a policeman leaned over and exchanged a few words with the driver.

Jim was at a *sobriety checkpoint*. With no advance warning, police select a random location and set up a roadblock. Every vehicle is pulled over. An officer observes the driver's mannerisms for any indication of drinking. Is his speech slurred? Does her breath smell from alcohol? Are any liquor bottles visible inside the car?

''How are you today, sir?'' the policeman asked Jim. The officer's eyes darted quickly around the interior of the car. He detected the smell of alcohol. Then he asked Jim, ''Would you pull off to the side, please?'' He pointed to an area on the other side of the roadblock.

The policeman asked Jim to perform the field sobriety test. Jim walked a straight line with no problem. He easily

touched the tip of his nose with his index finger. Without hesitation, he counted backward from ten. He showed no visible signs of intoxication.

The policeman then asked, "Will you blow into this little contraption?" Jim had the right to refuse, the officer informed him. If he did, however, he would automatically lose his license for one year under the implied-consent law.

Jim figured it was no big deal. After all, he had just passed the field sobriety test with no trouble. And he felt sober. So he blew confidently into the mouthpiece and – surprise! A .10 blood-alcohol level.

He was arrested for *Driving While Intoxicated (DWI)*.

At the police station, the Breathalyser matched the earlier reading on the preliminary breath tester. Jim was *booked* (officially charged) for drunk driving and placed in jail. Most drivers charged with DWI plead guilty. There is no defense against a Breathalyser reading of .10 or higher.

Jim was puzzled. He hadn't been weaving through traffic or speeding or driving carelessly. He had obeyed all the traffic laws. He'd had no trouble with the field sobriety test. How could he be charged with drunk driving?

The answer is simple. The law says that anyone with a blood-alcohol level of .10 or higher is legally drunk – no ifs, ands, or buts.

The penalties for drunk driving depend on the circumstances. Was the driver involved in an accident? Was anyone injured or killed? Had he or she been convicted of drunk driving before? How many times? Were there any

These students may not know that people can be legally drunk even when they don't feel anything. All they need is a .10 blood-alcohol level to be considered drunk by law.

other traffic violations? How high was the blood-alcohol reading? Was the driver reckless?

A conviction may result in *license revocation,* a fine, or time in jail. Many drunk drivers spend ninety days, six months, or a year in jail. In some states, a second or third conviction results in a felony conviction. Sometimes this carries a mandatory prison sentence.

The sentences drunk drivers are given in other countries are even sterner: In Malaya, the men and women married to drunk drivers are put in jail with their spouses. A second DWI conviction in Bulgaria is the last—the penalty is execution. Second convictions aren't a problem in El Salvador. Drunk drivers are executed by firing squad for their first offense.

THE FASTEST WAY TO SOBER UP

Many people enjoy having a drink or two at a party. They may also assume they can sober up before driving home.

But this simply isn't so. There are no shortcuts to getting sober. The only way to do it is to let liver, lungs, and pores eliminate alcohol from the body. They can only eliminate about an ounce of alcohol in one hour. A cocktail (mixed drink), a twelve-ounce can of beer, and a five-

People who enjoy drinking often make the mistake of thinking they can sober up with a quick drink of coffee before driving home. The truth is that there is no way to rush alcohol out of the bloodstream.

23

ounce glass of wine each contain about one ounce of alcohol. So it takes the body about an hour to get rid of one drink. Someone who had two drinks in a row would have to wait about two hours before the alcohol was gone.

Many people make the mistake of believing coffee, fresh air, or a cold shower will sober them up. But scientists now know these techniques do not work. Coffee may wake up someone who is drunk, but it can't take alcohol out of the body. All a cold shower can do is make someone cold and wet. Like water, fresh air may be invigorating, but it won't sober anyone up.

The body can't be rushed. Time is the only way to get rid of alcohol and its effects.

It takes two hours for the body to get two drinks out of its system. This body is in for a long wait.

A TOAST TO WENDY

"New York City! Wow!"

Wendy's friends were excited for her. In five days, she would be leaving for New York to attend acting school. Ever since elementary school, she had dreamed of an acting career. Now, at 19, she was getting her chance.

Leaving her friends would be sad, though, especially her closest friend, Betty. On their last weekend together, Betty and Wendy decided to go to a movie. Wendy picked up her friend at eight o'clock. Betty wanted to stop by another friend's house.

"The movie starts at nine, Betty!" said Wendy.

"I know. But Jill is leaving for her cabin in the morning. Tonight will be her last chance to see you before you leave. Just a quick good-bye."

"Surprise!" everyone shouted when Wendy stepped through the door.

Wendy grinned at Betty. "I thought you were acting a little suspicious."

"We couldn't let you get away without a going-away party," Betty answered. "We even have champagne!"

Wendy had tried beer and wine a couple of times in the past, but she had never been much of a drinker. But this was her night.

Everyone clinked their glasses together in a series of toasts. "Good luck to Wendy!" Clink. "Friends forever!" Clink. "To our future movie star!" Clink.

26

Drinking plays a major role in many American celebrations. It also plays a major role in many American traffic accidents.

With each toast, Wendy took a swallow of champagne. It didn't really taste like liquor, she discovered. It went down smoothly. And it looked just like Seven-Up. So bubbly. Her friends kept her glass filled. They talked, played music, danced, and laughed over their good times together.

Shortly after midnight, the party broke up.

In the car, Betty chattered constantly. She was really tipsy, Wendy observed. Wendy, too, felt a warm glow from the champagne. After five minutes, Betty leaned back against the seat and dozed off. Until then, Wendy had felt fine. Now she began to feel strange. Maybe it's too quiet, she thought. She turned on the radio and rolled down the window. Fresh air might clear her head.

Ten minutes later, Wendy realized she didn't know where she was. She was lost. This is silly, she told herself. Maybe I should stop…call a cab—or my parents…She continued driving around, getting more confused all the time.

She found herself entering a freeway. At the bottom of the ramp a horn honked. Then another. Cars flew past in a blur. Suddenly there was a squeal of brakes, and a bridge abutment loomed before her like a gray wall. A tremendous force propelled her forward into the windshield. Then—nothing.

Betty escaped with minor injuries. Wendy survived, but her face was badly disfigured. Eventually she would have to have plastic surgery—in six months or a year, after the deep scars had healed. It looked as if her acting career was finished.

Drunk driving shatters more than walls and windshields. It also shatters careers, bodies, and dreams.

29

People who have lost friends and family to drunk driving have joined together to warn others of what can happen when people drink, or use drugs, and drive.

ORGANIZING AGAINST DRUNK DRIVING

In the past 15 years, a massive outcry against drunk driving has taken place. Several organizations have given voice to this anger.

The most influential group has been Mothers Against Drunk Driving (MADD). This group was founded in 1980 by Candy Lightner, whose daughter was killed by a driver who had been drinking. A 1983 television movie, *The Candy Lightner Story,* attracted a national audience. Membership in MADD increased dramatically following this program. MADD members are active in several ways. They provide assistance to victims of drunk drivers, monitor courtroom proceedings, work toward stricter laws and enforcement, and provide public education programs.

Candy Lightner, left, the founder of MADD, lobbies for laws that would restrict driving while drinking. Here she speaks in Washington with politicians Richard Lugar and Elizabeth Dole.

A billboard in New York gives new meaning to being "the life of the party."

Two other prominent groups in the anti-drunk-driving movement are RID (Remove Intoxicated Drivers) and SADD (Students Against Drunk Driving). The goal of all these organizations is to change society's attitude toward drunk driving from complacency to intolerance.

A man named Robert Anastas founded SADD in 1981. He was a teacher and a coach. When two of his hockey players were killed in separate drunken-driving accidents, he decided something had to be done. First, he alerted his students to the many teenage deaths caused by drinking and driving. Then he organized them. Since most teenage drinking takes place among friends, he reasoned that the problem would have to be solved by teenager themselves. Adults weren't usually present when teens were drinking.

Before long, SADD chapters formed in schools across the

Concerned citizens have created a new phrase – "DWI," driving while intoxicated – and have shown us what DWIs can do.

In 1981, a man named Robert Anastas realized that the people best equipped to solve teenage drinking and driving problems were teenagers. Together, they created SADD.

country. To any school requesting one, SADD provides a "starter kit." This kit consists of informational brochures, posters, banners, a film, and 400 Contracts for Life (written agreements between parents and children to call each other should they find themselves in a situation where either they or the person they are riding with has been drinking).

Now before they go to a party, a lot of kids name a designated driver — someone who will stay sober and safely drive them home.

When SADD was organized in 1981, over 6,000 young people between 15 and 19 had died in drinking-related accidents in one year. In 1985—just four years later— that number was reduced to slightly over 2,000. SADD and MADD had a great deal to do with this dramatic drop in deaths connected to drinking and driving.

The federal government has helped, too, by putting

pressure on the states. In order to qualify for federal highway funds, states must first pass certain anti-drunk-driving legislation. Two examples of such legislation are the .10 blood-alcohol standard for intoxication and the implied-consent law.

The work of these organizations generated considerable publicity in the early 1980s. The drunk-driving issue made the covers of leading newsmagazines and was the subject of a number of television specials. This publicity inspired tougher legislation and enforcement.

SOLUTIONS

Although tough laws may help get drunk drivers off the roads, they are not the ultimate solution. That solution lies not with government or with organizations like MADD. It rests with each individual.

Most people have trouble knowing if they have had too much to drink. And even if they are within the legal blood-alcohol limit, they can be unsafe drivers. A group of professional drivers who took part in a drinking and driving experiment said they wouldn't feel comfortable riding with a driver even if she or he had as little as a .05 blood-alcohol level. In other words, the experts agree even one drink can make a driver dangerous. They say the only sure way to prevent accidents is not to drive at all when you drink.

If a designated driver ends up drinking at a concert or a party, then many kids call a friend or a parent, or they take a bus or a cab.

The best way to do this is to plan ahead. If you know beforehand that you'll be drinking, appoint a *designated sober driver*—someone who will not be drinking at all that evening. This is a common practice in Scandinavian countries, where drunk-driving laws are strictly enforced.

If you end up drinking without planning ahead, there are still things you can do to prevent accidents. You can call a cab, stay overnight, walk, take a bus. You can make sure you have the telephone number of a taxi or a bus schedule in your pocketbook or wallet. And you can always carry enough money for a taxi or bus just in case.

The point is to do whatever it takes to avoid driving after drinking. Drinking and driving isn't like flunking a test. You can't count on getting a second chance.

Contracts for Life are for both parents and children. They promise to call each other for safe rides home – no questions asked.

Ultimately, the decisions are up to you. Will you try to stop friends from driving when they have been drinking? Will you ride in a car that might end up looking like this?

CONCLUSIONS

The first recorded automobile death was in 1899. Since then, approximately 2.5 million Americans have died in on-the-road accidents. One American dies every 12 minutes in a motor vehicle collision. As one senator observed, car accidents are "the nation's most serious health problem."

There are, of course, many different causes of car accidents. Weather conditions—fog, snow, rain, ice—often complicate driving. Vehicles malfunction. Brakes fail. Drivers fall asleep, speed, and make errors in judgment.

We cannot always avoid many of these conditions—like bad weather. But we can refuse to drink and drive. And we can do everything possible to prevent our friends from drinking and driving.

Everyone has the power to prevent accidents caused by drinking. Someday you will have the power to decide: Should you drink and drive? Should you try to stop drunk friends from driving? Will you make the decision that saves lives?

FOR MORE INFORMATION

For more information on the effects of drinking and driving, write to:

Mothers Against Drunk Driving (MADD)
669 Airport Freeway
Suite 310
Hurst, TX 76053

National Safety Council
Department PR
444 North Michigan Avenue
Chicago, IL 60611

Remove Intoxicated Drivers (RID)
P.O. Box 520
Schenectady, NY 12301

Students Against Drunk Driving (SADD)
110 Pleasant Street
Marlboro, MA 01752

GLOSSARY/INDEX

BLOOD-ALCOHOL LEVEL—*Percentage of alcohol in the blood. A reading of .10 or higher is considered legally drunk. 11, 13, 21, 38*

BOOKED—*Officially charged with a crime. At a booking, the suspect is fingerprinted, photographed ("mug shot"), and then put in jail. 21*

BREATHALYSER/INTOXILYSER—*Machines that measure the percentage of alcohol in the blood from a breath sample. A digital display records a numerical reading: .10, .15, .20, etc. 13, 21*

DESIGNATED SOBER DRIVER—*Someone who will not drink at all on a particular occasion and will do any driving. 40*

DWI—*Driving While Intoxicated. A legal charge resulting from driving with a blood-alcohol reading of .10 or higher. 21, 22*

FELONY—*Serious crimes such as robbery and murder are felonies. Felons often receive long sentences in prison. A drunk driver who kills someone may be charged with manslaughter or vehicular homicide—both felonies. 8, 22*

FIELD SOBRIETY TEST—*A driver suspected of being drunk may be asked by police to perform a few simple exercises to test coordination and mental alertness. Several commonly used procedures are: walking a straight line, counting backward, touching the tip of the nose with the point of the index finger. 11, 19, 21*

GLOSSARY/INDEX

IMPAIRED—*Not fully in control of one's coordination, reflexes, judgment, or other skills required to operate a motor vehicle safely. Some states have Driving While Ability Impaired (DWAI) laws. Generally, a charge of driving while impaired is not as serious as a DWI (Driving While Intoxicated) charge. 13, 17*

IMPLIED-CONSENT LAW—*When you receive a driver's license, you are giving your consent (even though you may not know it) to be tested at any time for blood-alcohol percentage. You are not asked for your permission. It is "implied." In other words, you have no choice. If you refuse to be tested, your license is automatically taken away. 13, 21, 38*

INTOXICATED—*Drunk. Inebriated. Legally, having a blood-alcohol reading of .10 or higher. 13, 21, 32, 38, 45*

LEGALLY DRUNK—*A quantity of alcohol in the blood, usually determined by a reading on a breath–testing device. In some states the figure .10 is often used to determine if a person is legally drunk. 11, 13*

LICENSE REVOCATION—*Legally taking away someone's driver's license. 22*

PERIPHERAL VISION—*The area surrounding your direct line of sight. The space just below, above, and to each side of what you are looking at. 16, 17*

PRELIMINARY BREATH TESTER (PBT)—*A small, hand-held instrument for determining blood-alcohol level.*

GLOSSARY/INDEX

Basically, a smaller version of a Breathalyser. The PBT and field sobriety test are used primarily to help police decide whether to make an arrest. 13, 21

REFLEX ACTION—*The body's ability to act quickly and without thinking. Athletes need quick reflexes. A motorist, especially, needs good reflexes in order to respond instantly to unexpected hazards. Alcohol slows reflexes.* 15

SOBRIETY CHECKPOINT—*A roadblock set up by police to apprehend drunk drivers. Every car is pulled over. Police question the driver and observe his or her behavior for any sign of drinking.* 19

TUNNEL VISION—*Loss of the ability to see the "periphery"—that is, the area around the point you are looking at.* 17